The Husband
I Never Knew

The Sins of the Fathers

Diane Roblin-Lee

foreword by

Dr. Melodie Bissell

Library and Archives Canada Cataloguing in Publication

Diane
    The husband I never knew : the sins of the father
/ Diane Roblin-Lee

ISBN 978-1-896213-08-8

    1. Diane--Marriage. 2. Child molesters'
spouses--Canada--Biography. 3. Divorced women--
Canada--Biography. I. Roblin-Lee, Diane, 1945- II. Title.

HV6570.4.C3S54 2009   364.15'36092   C2009-904293-2

© 2012 Diane Roblin-Lee
Second Edition 2025

PUBLISHED IN CANADA - September, 2012
                            Second Edition - Updated December, 2024
byDesign Media
www.bydesignmedia.ca

COVER DESIGN – Diane Roblin-Lee

Cataloguing data available from Library and Archives Canada

Introduction

The Husband I Never Knew was originally written disguised as
a story told to me by a fictitious woman I named Kari. My world
had been rocked by the horror of the sexual abuse of my son by
his paternal grandfather, and years later, the horrendous discovery
that my then husband, the son of the man who abused my son, had
molested my precious granddaughter. With no experience in such
matters, I fumbled the handling of the abuse of my precious ones
and all but lost my family in the process. Having failed to protect
my son and granddaughter, I determined not to allow evil to
destroy us without fighting back and somehow exchanging shame
for honour for them and building something helpful for others
out of the ashes of our experience. I had to do whatever I could to
protect other children and families.

I hesitated, however, because my family had already suffered
enough without having the added burden of exposure. To protect
them, I initially wrote as though the story had happened to
someone else because it had to be told. I refused to be trapped by
the silence that predators count on to hide their evil doings.

Now 13 years down the road from that first edition, I understand
things a bit more clearly. My efforts to protect my son and
granddaughter from curious eyes only added to their injury.
Those who have been abused need validation and recognition that
they have been terribly wronged. Their childhoods were stolen.
To give my family the option of privacy in certain circles, I have
changed their names but am stepping out personally to slay the
dragon of silence.

To give deeper perspective, my story is followed by my interview
with my ex-husband, following his release from prison.

Diane Roblin-Lee

Predator-Proof Your Family Series

By Diane Roblin-Lee

Booklet #1 – *Why All the Fuss?* ISBN 978-1-896213-00-2
Prevalence, Effects and Trends of Child Sexual Abuse

Booklet #2 – *Who is the Predator?* ISBN 978-1-896213-01-9
Identification – Warning Signs

Booklet #3 – *Predator-Proofing Our Children* ISBN 978-1-896213-02-6
Recognizing the Grooming Process
Parent/Child Education – When the Molester Strikes at Home

Booklet #4 – *Predators in Pews and Pulpits* ISBN 978-1-896213-03-3
The God Factor - Forgiveness?
How Dare They Call Themselves Christians?

Booklet #5 – *The Porn Factor* ISBN 978-1-896213-04-0
Are You Raising a Predator?
The Old Bottom Line - The Buck

Booklet #6 – *It's All About the Brain* ISBN 978-1-896213-05-7
Does Child Molestation Affect Brain Development?
How to Use the Brain in Effective Treatment

Booklet #7 – *When the Worst That Can Happen Has Already Happened*
ISBN 978-1-896213-06-4 Healing for the Victim
Parenting an Abused Child – Coping as the Family of a Predator

Booklet #8 – *Smart Justice* ISBN 978-1-896213-07-1
Community Response to Predators Who Have Served Their Time
Church Response - School Response - Restorative Justice

Booklet #9 – *The Husband I Never Knew* ISBN 978-1-896213-08-8
The true story of Diane Roblin-Lee, ex-wife of a man who, after 38
years of marriage, confessed to being a child molester.

Available on Amazon in Paperback, Kindle and E-Pub
Also available through Plan to Protect®
117 Ringwood Dr., Unit #11, Stouffville, ON CAN L4A 8C1
www.plantoprotect.com 1-877-455-3555

Foreword

by Dr. Melodie Bissell, CEO of Plan to Protect® Inc.

Diane is a very brave woman. She has taken the intensity of the pain she has experienced and redeemed it among the pages of this book.

Diane shared her story with me a few years ago. I knew it had to be told. In the telling, we see once again that God's righteousness and beauty triumph. Diane's story breaks my heart and continues to break my heart every day, but it also spurs me on to keep doing what I am doing...raising the awareness of abuse, protecting children and youth from abuse, being relentless in creating safe environments for children and young people.

I encouraged Diane to tell her story through this book. Initially we weren't sure if the family would be open to it. We prayed that Matt and the survivors would be willing for the story to be told. It is heart wrenching. It is raw and, at times, disturbing. I can't help but wonder if I would be brave enough to share with others the pain that Diane has experienced. In the pages of this book she humbles herself and exposes the difficulties in her intimate relationship with Matt, her painful journey of discovering he was engaged in pornography and her raw emotions when she learned that the man she had been married to for 38 years had been unfaithful and had molested two young girls. Diane acknowledges how naïve she was in trusting Matt – but would most of us not have been the same way?

This is a real story. It is about a family torn apart by selfishness, lust and sin. All the comforts and joys they once enjoyed have been destroyed.

But make no mistake: this is not only the story of Diane and Matt and the children who had their innocence stolen from them. It is not only a story of Matt's betrayal of the parents of his victims, caregivers and family members.

It is an amazing story of God's redemption and saving grace. It is a story of His mercy and forgiveness. It is yet another story of how God transforms the mess of this world and creates something beautiful from it.

This story is not yet ended. It is the story of a journey. We have yet to see the full picture of God's redemptive plan. Today the individuals are rebuilding their broken lives, even though the consequences of sin continue to impact them years after the abuse occurred. Although Matt has served his time in jail, Diane, the victims and her family will never be the same.

Diane is truly a beautiful woman who has not allowed the pain to cripple her. Every day she demonstrates how she is trusting the Lord and watching for another miracle. The survivors of abuse in this story are beautiful, forgiving people who are trying to make the world a better place from the ashes of their experience. God is continuing to weave his mercy and grace into the lives of each individual. God is once more the Victor!

Thank you Diane for taking this bold step of faith and sharing this story.

"But He knows the way that I take; when He has tried me, I shall come out as gold." Job 23:10 (ESV)

Dr. Melodie Bissell
CEO Plan to Protect Inc.
www.plantoprotect.com

6

Prologue

Children are the most precious creations in the universe. They are vulnerable little people, dependent on adults for every aspect of their environment. I think God made them so adorable so that we would just love looking after them.

When I became a mother for the first time, I had the most amazing experience of suddenly feeling like a mother not only to my first little son, but to all the children in the universe. Motherhood is an awesome privilege of caring, protecting and nurturing the little ones of the world. I'm sure fatherhood carries the same feeling of loving not only one's own children, but having a sense of responsibility to any child anywhere who comes within one's sphere of life. We want children to be happy, to be safe and to grow strong.

Unfortunately, not all men and women have that deep sense of motherhood and fatherhood. Today, many have soaked their souls in pornography and walk around like ticking time bombs, waiting to act out the depraved fantasies that have been planted in their heads. Sexual child molestation almost invariably begins with someone dabbling in pornography, never in their wildest dreams intending to molest a child.

Had a plan for the protection of children, such as Plan to Protect™ been implemented in the church we attended, there's a good possibility that my family would not have been shattered, and my son and granddaughter and others victimized by my ex-husband would not have had their lives changed forever through abuse.

The following pages unwrap the story of the tragedy of my family in the hopes that witnessing the devastating outcome will make any potential predator think twice before touching a precious child inappropriately.

1
one

My Story

It was dark that cold January night. Friday the 13th ...not that I've ever been superstitious. It must have been about nine o'clock. I imagined my husband, Matt, to be downstairs in his studio working on a project, but was delighted to hear the voice of our pastor, Rob, joined with Matt's as their footsteps approached my home office. It was a cosy sanctuary in which I had written articles and books for over twenty-five years.

What was Rob doing here? Having turned my office chair toward the two men to say hi, I had barely gotten the word out before Rob shook his head solemnly and said Matt had something to tell me.

There was no warning – just a sudden torrent of words from my husband. "I did it! I did it all – and more!" Years of bottled secrets suddenly uncorked with the pressure of fermented evil. Incomprehensible sentences erupted from Matt's mouth in shocking ejections.

As the toxic words hit my brain, pushing to penetrate, I stared blankly at Matt. "You did *what*?" I didn't understand what he meant.

"I did it all – everything Sofia said – and more. More than anybody knows."

As the two men stood facing me, the only thing that registered was that, for the first time for as long as I could remember, Matt was looking directly into my eyes.

❧

It had been the week from hell. It had started early Monday morning with a call from my sister, Lisa, an hour's drive away.

"Diane, I need you to come. I can't talk about it on the phone, but I need you. I'll explain when you get here." She sounded very upset.

Without a question, I said, "I'll be there as fast as I can." It was unlike Lisa to make such a request. No drama queen, she had always been a solid and reliable anchor for me. Her life had always seemed relatively predictable – a successful career as a kindergarten teacher, a stable marriage, a son and a daughter, three adorable grandchildren and now, a relaxed retirement. What could possibly be wrong? Could her husband have suffered a heart attack? All I knew was that it must be serious for her not to tell me over the phone.

Flying as low as I could over the back country roads, I reflected on the difference in our lives. While Lisa's had been relatively tranquil, mine had been like a long-running soap opera.

I had been the rebel, the focus of prayer for my Baptist minister father and godly mom. Having gone as far from home as possible for my Acadia University years, I had become a Social Worker after graduation and then a high school Phys. Ed. teacher.

Anxious to get his high-spirited child settled down, my father had pushed hard for me to marry a young man who pursued me relentlessly. Matt's parents had Baptist roots and, with his own sporting goods business already underway, from Dad's perspective, Matt appeared to have what it would take to look after me comfortably.

Handsome, intelligent and outdoorsy, Matt quickly became a large presence in my life; picking me up from my office and taking me to nice restaurants for lunch, showing up at my apartment with surprises, keeping me stocked with fresh cut flowers and generally occupying my time.

While his attentions were flattering, it seemed to me that we were too different to become seriously involved. I enjoyed sitting with friends discussing interesting topics, going to parties, listening to classical music, exploring woodsy trails, dancing and all kinds of outdoor sports. Matt, on the other hand, seemed uncomfortable in group situations and preferred watching television to relating to people. Nevertheless, I enjoyed his family and his outdoor activities so much that I lingered in the relationship.

But there was that troubling business of the pornography. One day, while at his parents' home, I had opened the doors under Matt's bathroom sink and discovered a pile of porn magazines. Disturbed, I asked his mother whether she was aware of them.

Diverting her attention to something on the other side of the room, she turned away and shook her head in disgust. "I don't know why he reads that stuff," she muttered. It was obviously a taboo subject. I never discussed it with her again.

And then there was that slightly troubling discomfort I felt with Matt's dad. But he was charming, successful and respected by everyone. I tried to shrug it off as my own silliness.

Squeezed between my father's enthusiasm and that of Matt's

parents who both enfolded me warmly into their lives, I finally agreed to marry Matt, thinking it would make everyone happy and I could make it work. We had known each other for six short months before the big day. There were no false pretenses. All along, I made it very clear to Matt that I didn't love him. He assured me that it was okay, that my love for him would grow.

The night of the wedding rehearsal, reality showed up. I turned and went running back down the long aisle. I was all the way across the parking lot before Matt caught me. Catching me by the shoulders, he said, "What are you doing?"

"I don't love you. How can I marry you?" I agonized.

"You will. I promise you will."

With awareness of all the guests coming from afar for the wedding the next day, the dress Mom had made with all the covered buttons down the back, the wedding cake Dad had iced and the expectations swirling around me, I walked back to the church. After the rehearsal, I told Lisa she needed to come for a drive with me. I drove and cried until three a.m., not caring that we were lost in the maze of downtown Toronto neighborhoods. The next day, I combed my hair, donned my beautiful dress, popped a Valium and entwined my arm in that of my uncle and walked the long aisle where my father, who was officiating, and Matt, waited. Aunt Jessie, on the organ, said she had never seen such a happy bride. Little did she know I couldn't stop smiling because the Valium had made my mouth so dry that my lip would have gotten stuck on my teeth if I'd dared to close my mouth. I'd have looked like an idiot.

Three days into the marriage, it became apparent that Matt's effusive ardor had been nothing more than a manipulation to secure my commitment to him. He was not interested in the normal development of relationship. I was an object, a possession – in his words in later years, his "trophy wife." It was increasingly clear that he had married me for his benefit – not for mine. He was somewhat of a loner, satisfied with self-absorption.

When I became pregnant with Lucas after a year, I tried to fill my emotional void with my adorable son and the happy support of Matt's family. While my own family was just as thrilled about their grandchildren, they were wrapped up in their church and the spiritual aspects of life. Unable to relate to their priorities, I allied myself with the secular interests of my in-laws and became emotionally dependent upon them.

When at home, alone with Matt, I struggled with his lack of interest in intimacy. We lacked any deep heart connection. There was no pillow talk. When he would roll over to go to sleep, he would switch his bedside radio on to a talk show and become inaccessible. I would lie in the dark, feeling trapped and alone, often sobbing myself to sleep. He didn't seem interested in me as a person. When I would try to engage him in setting goals for our family, he would indicate disinterest, saying that he preferred to live more spontaneously. When I would try to involve him in purchases for our home, he made it obvious that he would prefer that I just go ahead and do what I wanted to do.

He was content for us to live parallel lives. Whenever we came to intersections where our paths had to join, like at Christmas or other special occasions, he was there, but was contained within his own walls. He could be very social and charming, but always at arm's length, never really letting anyone in.

I couldn't figure it out. He had pursued me as though I was the world's greatest treasure – and then, nothing – as soon as that ring was on my finger. It didn't make sense. I knew *I* hadn't changed. I bought book after book, trying to unravel the mystery. I remember finding one called, *Men Who Can't Love*. I could hardly wait to get home and read it, thinking it would explain my situation and I'd have the key to fixing it. More disappointment. I dug out my university psychology and sociology books, trying to find a name for the problem. Nothing fit.

Instead of disappearing after marriage as Matt promised it would, the pornography followed us wherever we lived. I would find it hidden in the most unlikely places. One day, I took the bathroom drapes down to wash and there were some porn novels, lined up neatly, perched on the top of the window frame. Sometimes the magazines were hidden amongst other magazines, sometimes between the mattresses. It infuriated me that he would bring such degrading, perverted material into our home where I was trying to provide a healthy atmosphere.

Determined to provide a healthy home for little Lucas (before Lincoln was born), I found out where Matt was getting the novels, went there and purchased one. Then, with my three-month-old baby in a baby seat, I strode into the police station and asked to see the chief. Ushered into his office, I introduced myself, proceeded to place my child on his desk, facing him, and placed the offending book on top of some papers beside my child. "Sir," I said, "how do you expect me to raise my little boy with any sense of nobility in this town, when you are allowing filth like this to be sold in one of your stores?" Obviously flustered, the chief picked up the novel, turned it over, read the blurb on the back, rifled through the pages, apologized and promised to look into it. I thanked him, picked up my son and went home. I later discovered that he was a user.

The pornography made me feel inadequate, devalued and objectified. Whenever I would confront him, Matt would apologize and promise not to buy anymore. The next batch I found would be more creatively hidden.

And then I came down with a case of mononucleosis. So exhausted that I could barely hold Lucas, let alone feed him, I was prescribed bed rest for six weeks. How does one lie in bed for six weeks and care for a three-month-old child? Because Matt was away a lot with his work, his parents offered to have Lucas and me stay at their home and they would look after us until I recovered. It seemed to be a wonderful solution for which I was most grateful.

They installed me in a bedroom on the main floor for easy access to care for me. Matt's father, Russell, was incredibly helpful, towing little Lucas around with a rope tied to a box, sitting by my bedside reading to me, pampering me with goodies, giving me back rubs...and then, after about two weeks, his back rub went askew and his hands went where they should not have gone. His wife, who I loved, was in the kitchen baking cookies.

I was horrified and paralysed by shock. I immediately blamed myself for being too accessible, too tempting, too alluring. I was 24-years-old and in the prime of my youth. It had to be my fault. My mind was a jumble of confusion. I dared not tell anyone because it would be devastating to Matt's mom. It would ruin their family.

That began three years of my mind being totally messed up. More than once, the thought of ending my life emerged. It was my love for little Lucas that kept me getting up, day after day.

We moved to Beaconsfield, Quebec, and it wasn't long before a friend informed me that my husband was being unfaithful. When I confronted him, he admitted to several office situations and disclosed an affair with a model from Utah who was moving east to be in the same city where we were living. Of course I told him that was the end of our marriage and prepared to move back to Ontario, closer to my parents. However, once again, he declared his ardent love for me and asked for my forgiveness, promising never to stray again.

Once again, I agreed to give him another chance. By this time I was expecting Lincoln and if there was any way I could keep our home intact for our children, I wanted to do it – but I could no longer live with the secret of Russell, his father, and called Matt home from work one day to tell him. One would expect fury from a man learning of the horrendous betrayal of his father, but Matt didn't react. He did nothing and life went on.

I adored my little boys and loved being a mom, doing everything I could to make their childhood wonderful. While there were some enjoyable trips and lots of fun times with good friends, I always felt that I had to work at keeping Matt's spirits up. If he didn't like something, he would simply retreat or go home and the good times would be over. It was like a ball game where the person who owned the ball would suddenly pick it up, take it and go, leaving everyone else unable to play anymore. And so I paid the price, constantly encouraging him and making our home as happy a place to be as possible. I would go to the park with my little boys and push them on the swings, watching other young couples with their families, wishing my husband was with me, too. I was so lonely.

I would go on like this for long periods, trying to mask my growing depression. And then I would erupt. I could play Susie homemaker for several months at a time, seldom complaining, always trying to make things work, but my real feelings and needs would build and build and build and build until BOOM! A piece of straw would break the camel's back and I'd get everything off my chest at once. Matt would listen and then walk away, lie down and read a book. He almost never argued. Despite my frustration, I'd always begin to feel badly about some of the things I'd said and, with the harmony of our home my greatest value, I'd go to him and apologize. Things would return to normal and we'd go on until the next eruption a few months down the road. For ten years, I struggled to make the relationship work, despite my loneliness and sense of entrapment. In all fairness, I know that he tried too, from time to time, but he was never willing to really engage with me.

Suddenly, one April evening, after ten years in the marriage, I gave up. I packed suitcases for the boys and me, put my dog and the boys in the car and left. We stayed with Lisa and her husband for a week, during which time Matt called several times a day, promising the moon if I would just return home.

Little did I know that my mom and Aunt Jessie had been fasting and praying for me every Monday since January that year. During that week away, I experienced a spiritual epiphany. Where I had been questioning the purpose in life and wondering how I could go on, day after day if this was all there was to life, I began to have a tremendous sense of God being with me and knowing that something enormous was changing. I began to dig into Lisa's Bible like a dehydrated nomad who had suddenly stumbled on an oasis. My once discarded faith found new life as a real relationship with God began to develop.

With a particular alignment of circumstances, eight-year-old

Lucas and five-year-old Lincoln, the dog and I went home at the end of the week, not intending to stay, but were talked into giving Matt another chance – again.

I tried to explain my spiritual journey to Matt and he basically had no problem with it as long as I didn't push it on him. However, seeing the enormous changes in my attitude and responses to life, he could see that something real was going on and, within a couple of months, he, too, began to search for relationship with God and experienced a conversion from secularism to Christian faith.

To me, this was heaven on earth. I thought we had finally found the answer. Now we were singing off the same song sheet. I definitely saw changes in him. He was more gentle, more relaxed and more comfortable with vulnerability. He seemed like a new person with whom I had to become acquainted all over again. We went to a number of weekend marriage retreats and gradually learned more and more about how to build a successful marriage. Matt actually seemed interested. We were building stability in our home. He became very thoughtful, doing things like warming my car up for me on cold winter days, helping with dishes and looking after basic chores. Pornography and infidelity were things of the past – I thought.

My main concern, during those years, was for Lucas, who often seemed depressed and out-of-sorts. It didn't make sense to me because he seemed to have everything he needed to be a happy child. He was intelligent, handsome, well-coordinated and lacked nothing materially – and yet he walked with his head down and his shoulders slumped. I couldn't understand it and didn't know what to do. More than once, I found little notes in his handwriting saying that he didn't want to live. I took him to a couple of doctors who found no issues.

100 Huntley Street had recently started broadcasting and I couldn't get enough of the wonderful stories of God's grace-ful intervention in lives. I began to write and had my first book, *My Father's Child,* published. When Matt established his own video production studio, "Praise Productions," I assisted him with accounting, sales and productions. I worked hard, trying to give my precious sons a name to be proud of and to train them to be people of character and integrity who would truly contribute to their eventual communities.

For the next (and last) 28 years of our marriage, Matt and I lived as Christians – I thought. Compared to the first 10 years of struggle, things were much better between us. We threw ourselves into the work of the church. Matt had a rich baritone voice and began to be asked to sing here and there. He led the praise and worship in the church we helped plant and I played the piano. He was elected to the church board. We organized and led a children's group and he did a wonderful job of leadership. The kids all loved him and he worked well with the helpers. As our sons got older, we began to lead a youth group, holding it in our home Saturday nights. There were often 40 or 50 teenagers in our huge family room with special speakers, interesting events or times of just hanging out playing pool, ping-pong, darts and whatever. We both taught Sunday School and hosted adult Bible studies in our home.

When Lucas was 12, in an emotionally charged moment, he confided to Matt that his grandfather, Russell, had been molesting him for years. When Matt told me, I was beyond devastated. This was why my precious Lucas had been suffering. I knew Matt's dad had issues because of what he had done to me, but I never dreamt, in my wildest imaginings, that he would touch a child. He appeared to be the best grandfather on the planet. Again, I expected the normal fury a father would express when faced with the worst kind of betrayal from his father. But Matt was immobilized and left it to me to handle.

I took Lucas to McDonald's the next day and, over a Happy Meal, told him what his grandfather had done to me. I wanted him to know it was safe to tell me, and he did. We were together in our sadness. He was not alone. Now I had to find the way forward.

Never having had any experience with child sexual abuse, I had no idea how to handle it. My primary concern was for my son and protecting him from any further damage. I called the police anonymously to find out what would happen if I reported the abuse. When I discovered that Lucas would have to testify against his grandfather, I thought it would place him in a very painful position and so didn't proceed with the police. I tried to shield him from the possibility of people finding out because I didn't want anyone looking at him as though he was 'different.' He'd already had so much stolen from him and I wanted to maintain whatever sense of normalcy there was in his childhood.

It seemed to me that because the root cause was sin, the transformation of Russell's heart would accomplish more than a jail cell. He and Matt's mom had mocked our conversion to Christianity and we had been praying for them for several years. So I went to a Christian bookstore and purchased a Bible and several books that I believed would speak to Russell's heart. I called him to meet me at a restaurant. Wired with a microphone in case it didn't go well, once we were seated and he asked me why I wanted him to come, I said, "I understand you have been molesting my son for years."

"Oh Di," he said, "I would never, ever do such a thing."

I replied, "On top of everything else you've done, are you going to try to make my son into a liar?"

He lowered his head and admitted it. I told him he would not be allowed to see his grandsons until he got himself right with God. I handed the bag of books to him with the bill, which I required him to pay. It was $78.05. He paid and we parted.

That was Thursday. On Saturday, I went to a nearby women's conference, leaving Matt home with Lucas and Lincoln for the day. My heart was broken. I never thought I'd smile again.

At noon, while the other women were having lunch, I got in my car and drove at crazy speeds over the flat and dusty country roads. I screamed at God, crying,"Why did You allow this to happen to my son? Why didn't you protect him?" Finally exhausted, I pulled over and stopped the car. My Bible was on the seat beside me. I picked it up and said, "There is NOTHING in here that can fix what has happened." I flipped it open in anger and despair – and there was the story of Hezekiah. It was as though it had been written just for me at that moment. I sobbed, knowing God was with us and would carry us through.

I went home after the afternoon session to discover that Russell had arrived shortly after I left and had asked Lincoln if he could speak with Lucas and his dad. He told them about having read Andrew Murray's book on prayer and how he had gone out in the woods and asked God to forgive him. He asked their forgiveness and they prayed together. I'd like to be able to say that his life was transformed but, sadly, as time went on, it proved to be another manipulation, Within two years, he contracted cancer and died with his Freemasons ring still on his finger.

If I had it to do over, I would have immediately called the police and requested that the law deal with Russell. As much as I had thought I was protecting Lucas, I actually prevented the carrying out of justice for my son. But that is hindsight. Now all I can do is share our story and urge anyone in a similar situation to involve the law. And that is why I'm sharing.

Little did I know that the introduction of the Internet in our home had kick-started the pornography again. This time, no books had to be hidden. It was just a matter of logging on when I wasn't around.

Instead of truly submitting his life to God and allowing Jesus to cut out the gangrene of his heart, Matt had retained control of his life and just used Him as a band-aid to cover the evil that remained, temporarily dormant, below the surface.

When an emotionally disturbed adolescent foster child with a history of sexual abuse flashed her breasts to Matt one day, the band-aid fell off and everything within him that he had allowed to remain dormant, rose up to meet the opportunity. From that millisecond of choosing to respond to that young girl with the darkness in his heart, Matt set all of our lives on a course that we could never have imagined. For 25 years, he kept the secret, knowing that if he disclosed his crime, life as we knew it, would be over. Of course I was oblivious to all of this.

Lucas got caught up in a teenage romance with a troubled girl and married at the ripe old age of eighteen. After eight years of marriage, and three children, two girls and a boy later, our daughter-in-law left.

Then began ten years of Matt and me struggling to assist our son in the raising of our grandchildren. It was a rough road, but we were a team – I thought. My estimation of Matt grew enormously as I saw the way he dug in, helping with Emma, Sofia and Tobias in an amazing way. He had no problem with driving them back and forth to school everyday, a two-hour per day commitment. Whenever they wanted friends over to play, he was happy to be the chauffeur.

Sofia was a beautiful child with huge brown eyes, long golden-brown curls and a tentative smile. As the middle child, she always had a special place in my heart. Her only apparent flaw was a chronic difficulty with telling the truth. Lucas and I had had numerous discussions about it but were at our wits end to figure out how to erase such a critical character issue.

The real love I had never felt for Matt grew as I developed a deep appreciation for his care for my grandchildren.

❧

Finally, walking up my sister's front path, I knew the suspense would soon be over.

As she greeted me, Lisa seemed almost incapable of speaking. "What happened?" I had to ask. "Just tell me."

"Diane, I... I... Sofia has accused Matt of molesting her. She told Lucas and Lucas called me to lure you away from the house so that you wouldn't be there when the police arrived to arrest Matt.

Everything within me constricted as icy tendrils squeezed my lungs flat. "That's ridiculous," I said.

Sofia was now 14-years-old. Because her mother had made no secret of her disdain for us and had been ruthless in her efforts to undermine us and ruin our relationship with Lucas and our grandchildren ever since we supported Lucas in his efforts to raise his children, the only possible straw I could grasp was the possibility that she had put Sofia up to the accusation. It didn't even enter my mind that Matt could be guilty. "I've got to call Matt!" I began to fumble for my cell phone.

"You can't," Lisa said. "Lucas said if you do, the police will pick him up right away, before they've had a chance to properly question Sofia, because they think he could be a flight or suicide risk."

"That's crazy," I said. "I've got to talk to him – I have to warn him about what's happening!"

"If you do, you're going to make matters worse. Let the police go through whatever process they have. Lucas said the police will call you here as soon as they've had a chance to talk to Sofia and Matt."

And so I waited – all day long, unable to speak, hardly breathing – until finally, at 8:30 that Monday night, the phone rang and it was Constable someone-or-other.

"Diane?" The voice was feminine, but matter-of-fact. "We have spoken with both Sofia and your husband. He claims he is totally innocent. We're going to drive him home. You can meet him there. Do you wish to speak with him?"

Suddenly, after the agony of forced separation throughout the day, it was Matt's voice on the line. He sounded tired and utterly dumbfounded – as I had expected. "I have no idea why

Sofia would say anything like this," he said. "It makes no sense! As soon as they told me what the charges were, I asked them to do a lie detector test on me, but they apparently don't do them here. They say if I want one, I'll have to order it privately."

That did it for me. When Matt said he had immediately requested a lie detector test, I had no shadow of doubt that he was innocent. A guilty man doesn't request a lie detector test. Little did I know he was aware that they wouldn't do one because it couldn't be used as evidence. Another manipulation.

Bidding a quick good-bye to Lisa, I rushed to my car. It was dark. I had lost the entire day. Speeding home over the dark, snowy roads I had travelled a gazillion times, I suddenly realized I was lost. Nothing looked familiar. I didn't have a clue which way to turn. Turning around, I retraced the icy roads, hoping I would find where I had gotten off track. After about twenty frustrating, lost minutes, I untangled the way.

Finally turning into the circular drive of the dream home in which we had lived for 26 years, I sensed a cloud of foreboding enshrouding our lives. A police cruiser was parked in my spot. The air was electric with intrusion and danger. How would we survive this terrible accusation? We had no experience with the dark side of the law. We had always enjoyed the security of those who live in harmony with the system.

Two officers were inside with Matt, searching the house for firearms, a routine exercise (I discovered) when someone has been charged with a crime. Matt had no idea where to find the key to the cabinet holding the clips and the registration papers for the hunting rifles that had been willed to him by his father and mine. I suddenly realized that our lives were no longer our own. We were subject to the demands of these uniformed strangers in our home. It was a different sort of home invasion. Shaking, I found the key and supplied the necessary paperwork.

Finally, the officers went out the door with the firearms and ammunition. We were left to look at each other in stark horror. Seeking comfort, we embraced, our silence electric with fear. There were no words for the questions. We were living an unspeakable nightmare. For the next four days, we neither ate nor slept, except in fitful moments of exhaustion.

First thing Tuesday morning, I arranged for a private polygraph test which would prove Matt's innocence to Lucas. Matt seemed as eager as I was for him to have it. The earliest available booking was for the following Sunday.

I then set about to secure the best criminal lawyer I could find, the associate of a close friend. Over the phone, he instructed us to compile every scrap that could possibly help with the case and meet him on Wednesday morning.

On top of having to go to the jail to give a statement to the constable somewhere in the midst of those horrific days, I had a deadline on a book that had to go to the printer on Friday. My mind felt like an over-extended elastic band.

When Lucas called my cell phone as Matt and I drove to the lawyer's on Wednesday morning, it was abundantly clear that there was no question in his mind about the truth of Sofia's story. I, on the other hand, despite my love for Sofia and concern for Lucas, had no doubt of Matt's innocence. Lucas was infuriated that I would believe Matt over Sofia. The lines were drawn. There was no slack – no space for discussion. We could expect no merciful turnaround. There was no waking up from the nightmare. The die was cast.

"You're dead to me." Lucas slammed the phone in my ear. It was a grey January day. We drove past snow-muddy fields bordered with rusty wire fences. The phone lay silent in my limp hand.

Matt said, "When we meet with the lawyer this morning, it's really important for me to have a totally clear conscience, because if there's anything not totally on the up and up, he'll probably read it and think I'm guilty – so I have a few things that I have to tell you to clear my conscience. Do you think you can handle it?"

"Handle what?" I asked.

"Well, I've had a few affairs that you didn't know about."

"With whom?"

"Well, Jillian, for one."

Jillian and her husband had been our best friends before we became Christians. Suddenly I was hearing that whenever Matt went on business trips to Toronto, Jillian faked business trips with her work and stayed with him. Nice friend.

"And then there were some stewardesses ... and remember that girl who worked with me when we lived in Beaconsfield and she came and stayed at our house when we had her doing some work for us...well, her. She stopped the affair with me though, because she really liked you and said I should work on our marriage."

I watched the fields go by on my side of the road. Such a sloppy winter day. At least the roads weren't icy.

"Are you okay?" Matt's voice was tender, caring – the tone for which I had longed through so many lonely nights.

I was numb. But okay – this was all garbage that had happened prior to us becoming Christians. It was stuff from the first ten years of our marriage when everything was so screwed up. So okay, I could handle it. Matt was a different person now. He was a Christian. His transparency actually reinforced my conviction of his innocence.

I said, "I don't like hearing it and I'm numb about Jillian, but none of that has anything to do with us now. It's over and we have to get through this thing. Once you have the lie detector test on Sunday, the truth will set everything straight."

Finally, we drew up to the lawyer's office and, armed with as much paperwork as we had been able to prepare for him, walked through the grey slush towards another new challenge. The only experience we had had with lawyers prior to this was with real estate and Lucas' divorce. What a mess.

Driving home, we felt somewhat heartened by the lawyer's assurances and directions. We had felt comfortable with him and had a sense that he really believed in Matt's innocence. It was comforting to have an anchor as the storm raged.

And now it was a waiting game until the lie detector test on Sunday. I could hardly wait for Lucas to see the results. Then the nightmare would be over and we could help him get some help for Sofia. He would feel terrible and the poor child must be going through hell knowing what a mess she was causing. I wanted to wrap my arms around her and tell her it was okay. We all do things in life we wish we hadn't done, that this was just a very hard way for her to learn how important it is to tell the truth.

Eating and sleeping were inconsequential. We couldn't. We tried to concentrate on the projects on which we had been working before all this happened, but focusing was hard. I spent a great deal of time in prayer and searching the Bible for passages to encourage Matt. I felt so sorry for him. He had been so wonderful to Sofia. How could she say such a thing?

Whenever I found a passage that was particularly appropriate and encouraging for Matt, I would type it out in large print, mount it in an eight by ten plastic frame and put it somewhere around his office where he could see it.

By Friday, there were about a dozen framed Bible passages sitting all around Matt's computer.

Still struggling to get my book finished to take to my publisher that afternoon, I was enormously relieved when he called, saying that his hard drive had crashed and there was no point in taking the book in until the following Tuesday. I'm not sure if there's an angel assigned to crashing hard drives, but if there is, I know where he was working that day.

All afternoon as I worked in my office, Matt was downstairs in his studio, surrounded by the framed Bible passages, working on a business project. Little did I know that one of those passages was messing with his mind, big time.

Finally, he could take it no more. It was over. He knew he had to confess. He knew he would never pass the lie detector test on Sunday and was struggling with great guilt for making Sofia out to be a liar. He had bluffed as far as he could bluff. He called Pastor Rob to come up to the house to be with us while he confessed.

❦

And now here we were in my office, with the toxic words of Matt's confession filling the air like a mushroom cloud. The world had stopped spinning on its axis.

When the eruption of his confession gradually settled into the ashes of our lives, I, feeling like a hollow caricature of my former self, stayed seated in the chair in which I had written, organized our lives and conducted the business of our family.

I had thought I had been dealing with reality all these years. Silly me. I stared at Matt, now so earnest in his confession, so open in his desire to connect, so visible with the evaporation of his walls. Now that I could see him, I didn't recognize him. He was a stranger. No one I had ever met before.

A tiny crack began to grow in the space between us. It widened and widened and gradually yawned into an uncrossable gulf. We were no longer connected. I was on my side of the abyss with my arms around the precious children he had harmed.

As Matt's words continued, spilling the dark contents of his mind into the canyon, they filled the horizontal plane, numbing me beyond any normal kind of pain.

Imperceptibly, something from above poured into me vertically, permeating my mind with a supernatural gift of forgiveness. It was that fast. As mercy met blame, it neutralized the power of bitterness with a preemptive strike, totally disintegrating its poised seeds.

The stranger standing in my office didn't look like the monster one expects a child-molester to be. He was my husband – but he was the embodiment of what happens to a human being when the most base inclinations are allowed to surface, roam around in one's mind and reach out with poisoned tentacles to destroy everyone within reach.

Everyone has dark inclinations, but living a life that contributes in a positive way to society requires a constant renewing of the mind with positive, healthy thoughts and appetites, not allowing any space for darkness to grow. Matt didn't live like that. He had gradually allowed the darkness in his heart full rein. He was human, but pathetically enslaved to evil desires.

As he stood there, I actually pitied him. He was like a prince who had signed over all the joys and riches of his kingdom for a soiled bag of deadly snakes. How could he be such a fool?

The natural response at that moment would have been to jump up and scratch his eyes out – but to this day, I have never experienced a vindictive kind of anger, despite the total shattering of our family. I have stumbled through deep, deep grief, but never vindictive anger. The anger that took root in me was far greater and deeper than anything that could be directed at a single human being. It was against the whole issue of child sexual abuse. While I have since become committed to protecting every child possible, at that moment, it was as though God anesthetized my emotions, my brain, my senses, with mercy. There were many people who declared that I was just going through one of the phases of trauma, but my feelings have not changed in all the years since that day. It had to be supernatural grace taking me through.

Thankfully, I had spent the previous 28 years of my life developing a relationship with God. I knew Him and He was with me. This was no time for scrounging around, trying to figure out who the real God was. My God had already stood up and made Himself known to me. I was not alone.

When the confession ended, Pastor Rob asked gently if I would like to go and stay with him and his wife, Liana. Prior to coming up to my office, Rob and Matt had called the police, asking them to come and pick Matt up, telling them of his guilt. Incredibly, the police claimed to be short-staffed and advised him to turn himself in on Monday. I knew I couldn't stay in the same house as Matt and so I gathered a few things and put them in a bag.

As Rob and I put our coats on and turned to walk to the front door, Matt was sitting on the wide steps leading from the foyer to the upstairs bedrooms and my office. Our big fluffy Old English Sheepdog, Bosley, sat beside him with his head in Matt's lap.

That was the last moment of 26 years in our beautiful home, 38 years married. While I had concern about leaving Matt alone in the throes of such trauma, I knew his welfare was out of my hands. He had chosen his past and his future and would have to deal with his present.

As I walked to the car, leaving everything familiar behind, I told Rob I had to see Lucas and Sofia right away. I had to make them understand how deeply I regretted not believing Sofia. How terribly, terribly wrong I had been. Rob called Lucas on his cell and arranged for us to meet outside, as it was very late and Sofia was already asleep.

As we stood in his driveway, Lucas wrapped his big arms around me and tried to forgive me. He had been through so much in the past five days. I ached with the understanding of our mutual inability to protect our children, and to have it happen at the hands of the people we should have been able to trust most in the world was soul destroying. The snow flakes fell through the darkness the same way they've always fallen, but in our worlds, nothing would ever be the same again.

❦

As we drove to Pastor Rob's home, primal groans from eons of antiquity rose to my lips, carrying with them the pain of humanity wounded by sin from the dawn of time. Words had no significance.

By the time we arrived, Liana had lovingly prepared a fold-away bed for me downstairs in their family room. Rob explained the television controls and Liana, fussing around, tried to interest me in some food. I couldn't eat.

Woodenly, I prepared for bed and then fooled around with the television controls a bit. I thought maybe if I could find Larry King, I might be able to muster enough diversion to quiet my mind. However, whether it was Rob's confusing instructions or my scattered attention, I couldn't get the television working. I was too distracted by trying to glue together shards of my broken thoughts.

Crawling under the soft blankets like a little child alone in a single bed, I remembered the warmed, fluffy white blanket they had placed on me in the hospital many years before, after 34 hours of hard labour giving birth to Lincoln. What comfort! I had kept that blanket with me for the whole five days in the hospital. Lying there in Liana's bed, I thought, "This must be what it's like when you've been hit by a truck and you lie on the roadside broken and bleeding and someone covers you with a blanket, saying, 'She's in shock.'"

All night, I lay awake, hardly blinking, staring at the ceiling. I asked God to show me how to handle the situation and what to do. From time to time, sobs erupted, not like the self-conscious weeping of an adult, but the uncorked crying of a wounded child.

No voice spoke to me from on high. No angel appeared with a

list of instructions – but three thoughts became more and more firmly embedded throughout the long night. I had to sell the house (which involved dismantling our business and dealing with a lifetime of work and possessions), I had to divorce Matt, and I needed to go somewhere to get some distance from the situation to get some perspective.

♣

In the morning, I declined Rob and Liana's kind invitation to stay for a few days, knowing it would just prolong the inevitable. I had to get back home to begin the rest of my life. Liana's mom insisted I take a bowl of chili with me. I was about to learn the magnified importance of little acts of kindness. Every one meant so much.

When Rob drove me home, Matt and our second car were missing. We immediately wondered if he had committed suicide. When the phone rang, it was the constable, saying that Matt had driven himself to the Police Station and turned himself in, confessing to all of his offenses, not just those charged by Sofia. There were now 13 charges and five victims, two of whom Matt had actually molested and three attempts. The constable wanted me to go to the jail and give a second statement. The next day would be fine.

Where was I in this mess? What label do they put on someone who has been deceived for 38 years? Victim? Is betrayal a crime? My life was stolen. Thirty-eight years of memories were defiled. Who would ever want to look at our family albums? None of those photos depicted the hidden underbelly of our home.

It was hard for me to understand why I was not angry. I should

34

have wanted to strangle Matt. Knowing others would expect anger and want me to hate him, I worried that they would misunderstand the lack of anger as my condoning of his actions. Nothing could be further from reality. Had I allowed anger to trump mercy and own my life, it would have been so monstrously huge that it would have destroyed us all. I chose mercy.

I couldn't rest until I could see Sofia to try to communicate the depth of my remorse for not believing her. When I knew she would be home from school, I went over to Lucas' house. She received me warmly and we sat on the chesterfield while I did my best to apologize. Her big brown eyes were soft and gentle. I felt we really connected that day. While my disbelief in her story had hurt her very deeply, she claimed to understand why I had not trusted her.

And then I went home and called my good friends in Florida who had been praying for us. A few minutes after hanging up from telling them about Matt's guilt, they called back, inviting me to fly down to stay with them for a couple of weeks. It was a welcome idea for distance and perspective.

That night, in my efforts to keep functioning, I tried to assess where I was financially. Despite the fact that Matt was highly regarded in his work, he had not marketed himself aggressively and relied on word of mouth for his clientele. Our studio, over a hundred miles north of Toronto, was too far removed from the city to be a serious contender for market share. We got by, but there was seldom much left over. At this point, he was in the middle of projects for three clients, all of whom had pre-paid the lion's share of the invoices. I would have to repay everyone and there would be no more income. With the housing market down, the equity in our house wasn't great. And then there were all the legal bills that would soon come pouring in...

Alone with my cats and Bosley, I looked in all the little catch-all places and rounded up the loose change. As I rolled the pennies, nickels, dimes and quarters, images of my husband sitting on a hard cot in a cold jail cell jack-hammered through my mind. My husband who always slept nested in a warm bed with nine pillows, all strategically placed for comfort – was alone. I knew he needed to be there. I wanted him to be punished – but where was my anger? I could find it only in the raw aching for the plight of the children. I rolled 47 dollars in change.

Other than the occasional padding around of the cats and the sounds of Bosley's presence, the house was quiet. Whenever Matt used to go away on business trips, I hated it because I was always fearful of staying all alone at night. I would turn on the television in my room so that I couldn't hear the sounds of the house and kept Bosley beside my bed and a dagger under my pillow. Now I was faced with a lifetime of being alone. I could live it in fear – or deal with it. I asked God to please look after it. From that moment, my fear left. I lived all alone, fearlessly, in that huge, rambling house for seven months until it sold.

❧

Following a fitful sleep, I got up Sunday morning, faced with the emptiness of life ahead and the horrible prospect of having to go to the Police Station to give a statement. Who was that person in the mirror? Was this really my life?

Sunday mornings had always meant church. Trying to keep moving, I couldn't think of any better place for a broken person to go. Mechanically, I applied my makeup, got dressed and drove the half hour to church. I went a bit late and slipped into a back pew. The news had already circulated and people were no doubt shocked to see me there. While I was conscious of a few furtive stares, it didn't matter. I had bigger things to worry about and their shock was understandable.

I wasn't the only one who had been betrayed by Matt. All of these people had been duped into believing he was a fine Christian man. They had trusted him around their children. If I had been clear-minded enough to consider all of the implications, I might not have gone to church, thinking it would spare the people the immediacy of the situation – but my mind was fixed simply on finding a spot as close to God as I could get.

I was grateful for the warmth and prayers of the people, but not yet ready to understand the fallout Matt's sin would have in the lives of many of these people and others in our circle of friends, associates and family. It's not uncommon for some people to assess the reality of Jesus by watching the lives of people who claim to be His followers, particularly people in leadership. I know of several precious souls who abandoned the faith, believing Matt's sin proved God was just an illusion. It makes me very sad.

After church, it was time to go to the Police Station to give my second statement. Some good friends kindly drove me to the station so that I would be able to pick up our second car, which Matt had driven to turn himself in. As we drove into the parking lot, there it sat, like a dog waiting for its master to return. In the cup holder, was Matt's wedding ring.

Once again, I walked up the steps to the Police Station. There were only three other connections I had ever had to a place like this. The first was as a little girl when I went with my minister father to arrange the release of someone he was trying to help. The second was when I had scheduled an interview with an incarcerated fellow for my first book. The third was my visit to the Chief – and now I was to give a statement concerning my child-molester husband.

When I entered the station, a man and a young teenage girl sat quietly waiting for who-knows-what. They looked like gypsies. The girl sat, half slouched, chewing her nails. The balding man, who appeared to be her father, was talking to her in hushed tones about her mother's problems with alcohol. The air was thick with sad stories.

Now I was a member of their club – people whose lives had somehow become entangled in the system. Trying to maintain some semblance of respectability, I approached the glass window and asked to see the constable.

This time, our taped conversation was considerably shorter than the first statement. While I had gone to great lengths in our first meeting to demonstrate the impossibility of guilt, this time it was just a pathetic recounting of Matt's confession.

🌿

On Monday morning, I drove to the courthouse to get the papers to file for divorce. I had a list: get a divorce, sell the house, go away for a couple of weeks to process my thoughts.

This wasn't going to be complicated. There were no custody issues and initially, I thought I could do it myself without increasing all the legal bills I already had. A woman with a kind demeanor and gentle eyes answered a few questions and helped me find the right forms. Kindness is golden in times of pain.

I kept waiting to wake up. All those years of meaning nothing to my husband could not have happened. Was I really starting divorce proceedings? Was my husband really sitting in a jail cell? Was he being beaten? How could he have done those things to Sofia and the other girls? What would all this mean to my sons and their families? How deeply would it destroy my desire to be a role model and influence others spiritually? What about the community – and the people in our church?

When I got home, I plugged myself into my computer and worked until 2 a.m., finishing the book I had to take to Toronto the next day. Every tiny detail in the layout was critical.

On Wednesday morning, our lawyer wanted Pastor Rob and me to be in court by 9:30 a.m. Matt was scheduled to be formally charged. Without Rob's understanding and support that week, I have no idea how I would have survived.

Before leaving the house, I had to admit three police officers who would stay the day while I was gone, searching the house and all of our computers for pornography. There were no scrolling credits, music or commercials. This was real life.

My journal records Wednesday, January 18th, 2006 as the worst day of my life. An excerpt reads,

My pain is so deep and raw that I can barely keep it covered with my skin. Sometimes I feel as though if I touch my skin, I'll break and there will be no stopping the flow of blood from my wound. But God is holding me.

Matt's only sibling, Sylvia, was ashen as she and her husband joined Rob and me at the court house. The four of us sat bundled in our winter coats on a hard bench, while the court proceeded with the business pertaining to the day's offenders.

When Matt's name was finally called, he was led into the prisoner's box in shackles. He was hunched and unkempt, wearing the same clothes he had had on for the last five days. They hung over his big-boned frame as though he had lost 30 pounds.

The man I had known – the handsome, confident, talented man – was reduced to a dishevelled, incoherent, sobbing shell. It's a terrible thing to see someone utterly destroyed, essentially by his own hand – particularly when that someone has been the father of one's children, the grandfather of one's grandchildren and one's husband for 38 years. When the judge suggested psychological testing needed to be considered to establish a plea, Matt was led out by a guard and the door locked behind him.

At the request of our lawyer, he and Rob and I were allowed to meet with Matt briefly in the cells below the courthouse to try to assist in the process of getting a coherent plea.

The cells below the courthouse, smelling of bleach and urine, were sparse and barren. Without so much as a magazine, the prisoners can wait on a hard bench all day to be taken upstairs for a couple of moments before a judge. At the end of the day, they are shackled together, loaded into a metal-benched paddy wagon and returned to the jail.

This was my first moment of speaking with Matt since the night of his confession at home. Now our only communication was by way of telephone receivers on either side of a bulletproof window in a tiny cubicle. The change in him was – I don't have a word. His skin was ashen and he was deranged, totally out of touch with reality. He was having a complete breakdown; listening for voices, instructing us to wait until he could hear answers from God, sometimes almost manic in joy and suddenly lost in agony and incomprehension.

At that point, Matt was flatly refusing all counsel and assistance of any kind. In lucid moments, he didn't feel he deserved any help. But it was important for him to have someone represent him who had experience.

From that incredibly disturbing meeting, Rob led me somberly out to his car and drove me home. By the time we arrived, about 4:30 in the afternoon, the police had finished searching the house for pornography and had found nothing, although all of Matt's computer equipment had been removed for intense screening. As I walked through the rooms, I was stunned at my loss of privacy. Even my underwear drawer and my cookbooks had been searched. Now that even my privacy had been invaded, what more, beyond my family, my memories, my business and our name could be taken?

I picked up one of the books I had written. Even my life's work was besmirched. After becoming a Christian, I had been so eager to share the wonderful things I had discovered that I had filled the years writing and speaking about the reality of God and His amazing ability to change lives. Now, because of Matt's crimes, people would say that God wasn't able to change people after all – that I was kidding myself.

I had tried to be an example for my sons, my grandchildren and my daughters-in-law. That was gone. If I couldn't even figure out the fact that my husband was a child-molester, what did I really know about anything? Since the passing of my mother, I had become the family matriarch, given the mantle of honor generationally passed to the eldest female in a clan. The title carries with it images of a woman who has gained the wisdom that comes from years of experience, surrounded by an adoring family. Gone. All gone.

As sad as the shredding effect was in my life, the repercussions in Sofia's life and in those of the other young girls, would follow like rips and discolorations throughout the tapestry of their lives.

And it wasn't just about the immediate victims. This was just the beginning of a long road ahead in healing for Sofia. I knew from experience what it was like to try to parent a child who had been sexually abused. Parenting Lucas through his teen years had been very challenging because his soul had been so wounded. Night after night I would go through a list of divine affirmations with him to try to repair what had been broken and strengthen what had been torn down in his heart. Gradually, thanks to lots of prayer and love and summers spent in the wonderful atmosphere of Circle Square Ranch, Lucas became strong and solid and developed an amazing resilience that has taken him through more challenges in his adult life than almost anyone else I know.

Because of what Lucas endured and what we had gone through with him, trying to help him heal, I had trusted my husband more with our grandchildren than I would trust anyone else. He knew first hand what the effects of abuse would bring, and yet had continued the generational sin of his father. How could he have been that disconnected?

The effect of Matt's crimes was particularly shattering to our sons and their families. It could not have been worse if a nuclear bomb had exploded in our midst. In the face of such a contrast between Matt's public persona and what he was doing in the darkness, it was difficult for some to retain their faith. While some remained solid, others floundered and looked to the world for diversion and comfort.

I know God isn't finished with our story. Broken hearts

are just part of a bigger picture. Shattered dreams are never random. While I wait for God to put back the broken parts, my challenge is to turn this nightmare into something helpful to others in similar circumstances. I love my family too much to have them shattered for nothing.

For that reason, although I failed to protect my own family, I have taken what we learned from our experience and turned it into something to hopefully protect other children and families from similar trauma. God's got this.

Hence the nine-booklet series, *Predator-Proof Your Family* and our LifeNet ministry. *www.lifenet4hope.com.*

🎕

2
two

Matt's Story

Following my decision to tell my story, I discussed the ramifications with Matt following his release from prison. Because it was not only my story, but his as well, I felt I needed his permission to share. Deeply remorseful, he was broken and totally open to exposing his deepest shame if it could in any way dissuade anyone else from targeting a child or acting on fantasies – or if it could in any way bring healing, insight or prevention into the epidemic of child molestation.

Once it was written, I knew his perspective would lend deeper insight for the protection of other children – if he would agree to having me interview him.

He agreed with no hesitation.

We met one cold, fall morning in my apartment. We sat on the furniture that had once belonged to both of us and graced our beautiful home in the country. Everything felt surreal as I plugged in my equipment to record the sad legacy of this broken man – the husband I had never known.

While not an example of a sadistic pedophile, my research showed that Matt is typical of a multitude of child-molester predators who started out dabbling in pornography and end up not only destroying the lives around them, but losing everything, making his story so relevant to today's culture.

Here, then, is Matt's story in his own words.

D. You were convicted and served time in prison for molesting two young girls and attempting inappropriate behavior with three others. How are you feeling about me telling the story?

M. If it helps somebody or keeps somebody from doing what I did, then it's good.

D. Let's go back to the beginning. Where did this all start? What was the root?

M. Pornography was certainly a major contributing factor.

D. Was there anything else at the root of it?

M. Well, the absence of a healthy adult sexual relationship was not a good environment for me to be in.

D. How do you account for that? Why couldn't you have a good sexual relationship with me?

M. I think that on our honeymoon when I was more open about wanting to do the kind of stuff I saw in pornography, and I realized that you weren't into it, I disconnected and took the easy way out in more pornography and fantasizing and other relationships. We just grew apart. Instead of working on a healthy relationship, I replaced normal, healthy sex with more and more degrading pornography.

D. So you had no desire for normal sex ?

M. No.

D. Do you think that if I had participated in all the things you wanted to do, you would never have gotten involved with the first young girl?

M. There's no way of knowing that. I never had any thoughts of kids. All the time I was messing around with other women while I was travelling so much, it was all about adults. The thought of kids never crossed my mind.

D. In terms of the root, do you feel that there was anything generational, or anything in you that led you to be attracted to children? Do you feel that you were born with that sexual predisposition?

M. I don't think so. Psychologists have determined that I am not a real pedophile. Not all people who molest children are pedophiles. True pedophiles just go for kids. That is not my preference. I was always into adult sex but got involved with the two young girls because they were there and I was so selfish that I cared more about self-gratification than anything else at the time. I think that in both cases, with both girls, it was a matter of convenience. I was in a trusted position for a long time.

D. When you were a child, did you have sexual experiences or were you molested by anyone?

M. When I was about nine, I was molested by a counselor at a Scout camp. I called home and tried to get my parents to come and get me, but they didn't and so I told the senior camp counselor. Then my parents came and got me. Other than that, there were about three instances of experimentation with other children who were older that I, but in talking with psychologists, they seem to think that those circumstances were just normal childhood curiosity.

D. *What did your parents say to you about it?*

M. We never talked about it. It was as though it never happened.

D. *Do you feel that had any effect on your sexual development or your relationship with me, or...*

M. I don't know. It wasn't a good situation. I felt very ostracized at the camp because I was treated like the snitch who had caused this fellow who molested me to be sent home. Everybody was mad because this fellow had been very popular. They didn't know what he had done to me. I just wanted to go home, to get out of there. I was there for about a day before my parents came.

D. *Do you, yourself, feel that the incidents with other children were normal childhood occurrences – or do you feel that they had an effect on your development?*

M. It's not something that you can qualify. I don't know what I would have been like had those things never happened.

D. *Research speaks of the "grooming process" child molesters use to gain the trust of their victims and families. Did you intentionally groom your first victim with the intent of molesting her?*

M. While I had begun to fantasize about schoolgirls, I never intended to actually get myself in a situation of molesting a child. The first time it happened, I was leading a children's church group and a young girl who was a foster child of a family in the church used to want to be around me all the time. She had been sexually active in a previous home and was very clingy with any male leader who would pay attention to her. She was mentally and emotionally weak and just wanted someone to love her. She wanted males to love her. One of the other leaders had to have a talk with her foster mother about how she was constantly making plays for the male leaders. I played on her needs. One day when I was at her home, she flipped her top up out of the blue and exposed her breasts to me. That's when I should have just told her to pull her top down and left the situation, but I didn't.

D. Did the foster parents not suspect anything?

M. The girl's foster mother was very observant. I felt she was always on the outlook for the kids because she had had a previous situation where someone was suspected of molesting one of her grandkids and so I never pushed anything, simply because that would have been a red flag to her. I could sense that she was always very protective.

D. Did you ever feel that she had any distrust of you?

M. No. Not at all. In fact it was exactly the opposite. I was very much in a position of trust with the kids.

D. You must have begun to feel very isolated after all that began to happen. You became isolated from people who could have helped you. Can you talk about how that was?

M. It just reinforced the behavior. It made me go deeper into unreality and interact more with the kids than with the adults. It was a real catch-22 situation.

D. How did you see yourself in relation to other people?

M. I always felt that in a funny sort of way I was superior to other people – that I was smart, that I was clever. I was getting away with it. Did I like me? No. But deep down I always felt that I did a good job at a lot of things. I felt that there weren't a lot of people who could do certain things as well as I could do them. Believe it or not, I thought I was spiritually astute. That was a total deception, obviously. I was proud to the extent of being vain. Not a very nice person. I worked at trying to appear to be a nice person, but it was all a sham.

D. How long did that situation with that young girl continue?

M. I'm not exactly sure. She eventually went to another home in Toronto. Then there was a church party of some sort and I volunteered to go to Toronto to pick her up and that's when it ended.

D. Why did it end?

M. Because I took her to a secluded spot on the way and proceeded to molest her and she started to cry. That's when I stopped. I snapped out of it and took her home.

D. There were quite a few years between the first girl and Sofia. Why did you choose Sofia?

M. I think Sofia was the most vulnerable. She was always very clingy and wanted to be around me. She was at our house a lot. Sofia was very bright, but she was emotionally needy because of her circumstances and she craved the attention. Other kids who were strong characters never entered my mind. Never even entered my mind.

D. How old was she when you began to touch her?

M. I think she was about ten. *(Note: According to Sofia, she was actually much younger.)*

D. Was she frightened?

M. No, I don't think so. It began as a back rub and just progressed from there. In my mind, she was enjoying the attention. I was obviously rationalizing totally inappropriate behavior. It was totally about self-gratification.

D. So her discomfort wouldn't have stopped you.

M. No. The best thing Sofia ever did was to tell, because even though I stopped over a year before she told, I'm convinced that I would have started again at some point.

D. Your desires were progressive, then?

M. Yes. I never went beyond touching the girls with my hands, but towards the end, I was fantasizing about being touched and I know I was moving in that direction.

D. When you were touching them, were you physically aggressive? Did you force yourself on them?

M. I did with Sofia. I wasn't violent, but I knew that she didn't want to do certain things and I did.

D. Would you have progressed as far as rape?

M. No, I wouldn't have forced her like that, but if she hadn't cried, I would have gone further and if she had given any inkling of wanting to participate – which I know was a ridiculous thought – I would have gone further. That's just how low my mind had sunk.

D. How old was she then?

M. She would have been twelve or thirteen. But in both cases, with both of the girls, when they cried and said stop, I stopped. I think when they cried, they broke through the veil of being objects to me and became children and that's when I stopped.

D. When you were molesting a child, how did you feel about the child?

M. I didn't really have any... I think I felt that I was giving them pleasure, or that was what I told myself, which was of course not true. It was all about self-gratification. While I was touching them, I really thought of them as objects, not as children. When you're doing that you don't think of them as victims. It's just as though they're nonexistent. They're not people. They're objects.

D. Did you ever have a real relationship with Sofia? Was she ever a human being to you – or was she always just an object?

M. Oh no, I cared very deeply for her. It was only when I was trying to self-gratify myself that she was an object. But there were so many times when I felt so close to her. I was almost like a Dr. Jeckyll and Mr. Hyde. I was very deceptive. Extremely deceptive. There are perpetrators who basically target a kid on the street and use violence but that wasn't my thing. It wasn't anything I ever did or would have done. There was always something deep inside of me that said that wasn't ever going to happen.

D. What were your thoughts after you had molested a young girl?

M. Regret. Deep, deep regret. I felt very unworthy. Like a real heel. A real schmuck.

D. So after Sofia cried, it never happened again?

M. That's right. It never happened again. And I think it was over a year before she reported me. If I hadn't gotten caught, I know I would have tried again. The victim needs to tell.

D. If she had been questioned, do you think Sofia would have told about it earlier?

M. I think that communication from adults to the child is extremely important, because I have a feeling that if anybody had sat down with Sofia and asked her if everything was okay in the relationship between her and me, I think she would have spoken up and said that there were some things going on. I doubt that she would have said anything to her teachers at school or whatever, but with someone she really had a relationship with, I think she would have said something if she had been asked.

D. Did you ever want to confess – and if you did, what stopped you?

M. Yes, I did, but fear wouldn't let me. I was trapped. There was nothing I could do about it without blowing my family apart – which has happened.

D. According to the research I've done, one of the characteristics of child molesters is that they don't pay attention to normal societal boundaries. Were you aware that you were breaking societal barriers, or did you just not care, or what?

M. I don't think I was aware that I was breaking societal barriers.

D. So you weren't aware that it was improper to go into a child's bedroom?

M. No. Not really. I was much more comfortable with children than with adults. I think it's because with adults you can't be totally open and honest, but with kids you can and I enjoyed that. So it was a lack of maturity. That and the fact that my guilt prevented me from being able to relax with adults.

D. Did you find that you could express yourself more with kids?

M. No, I would draw them out. I wouldn't talk about my deep feelings with them. I would just talk about them.

D. What would have stopped you from touching a child in the first place?

M. If they had said no. Saying no and crying. In both cases, with both of the girls, that was it. That was what stopped it with both of them. Now – will that stop every child molester? No. I don't think so. It's just that I have a soft heart and when reality sunk in that I was hurting this child, then I stopped.

D. Did you ever hear on TV or on the radio about the consequences of molesting a child?

M. All the time.

D. How did that affect you?

M. I'd just quiver and shake inside and be glad that I hadn't gotten caught.

D. But you proceeded anyway. Why?

M. Just lack of self-will. I'd just always make myself think, well, she appears to like it, so... I mean it was delusional, but that's what I did.

D. Did you want to be caught?

M. I wanted to stop. I didn't want to get caught. I just couldn't figure out how to stop.

D. Did you ever try to seek help in any way?

M. Yes. I would constantly pray that the Lord would get me out of it. I knew it was wrong and felt very guilty after the fact, but just wasn't strong enough to stop it.

D. So if you prayed that God would help you to stop, why do you think He didn't?

M. I think it was just a hollow prayer. It just wasn't sincere. My desire for what I was doing was stronger than my desire to stop.

D. How did you hide your sexual preferences all those years?

54

M. Just by being very manipulative.

D. *Did you feel guilt?*

M. Yes.

D. *How did you handle that?*

M. Just tried to put on a brave face – be someone I wasn't. Basically a mask. I couldn't ever really have an in-depth conversation with anybody for fear something would slip. There was no honesty in anything. It was very depressing. I just buried myself in work projects and so I was never really around anybody for long. I just kept working and working so I didn't have to think about it. That was my self-preservation mechanism.

D. *Do you think people have to be cautious when they see a strong bond between a man and a child?*

M. I think people have to be perceptive – not cautious – perceptive. For instance, I have a bad feeling about a fellow at my church now. There is a woman there who has two young daughters and a boyfriend. They left the church and he took one of the girls with him – not both girls – one girl. To me that was an instant red flag. I wondered why he separated those girls. So I think that if you want to protect a child, you have to watch how things are orchestrated and understand manipulation.

D. *When you questioned that, should you have confronted that, or should you have just let them go as you did and hope for the best?*

M. I am going to speak to the pastor about it, but I am in a very delicate position in that church. There are certainly people, I would say the majority of people, who are spiritually mature, rational people who understand the nature of forgiveness and are giving me a second chance. There are a few, however, who are really upset about me being there. They haven't actually vocalized their concerns to me, but I certainly sense the vibe. They have spoken to the pastor about it, but he's giving me a chance. It's a hard situation.

D. *So you feel that in your position you really can't address it. But for someone else who was concerned, do you feel that the fellow should have been challenged?*

M. Well, it was with the full approval of the mom. She went out to his car and opened the door for the little girl to get in and then let them go off on their own. I guess that in my situation right now, I'm just paranoid. I could be over-reacting to this situation with the mother and her boyfriend, because friends of the pair, who seem to be people of good judgement, don't appear to have a problem with it. They seem to think it's okay. Anyway, a parent just has to be wise.

D. *Did you ever feel that there was any kind of demonic presence influencing you or harassing you or whatever?*

M.. No. I think Satan gets blamed for a lot of things he doesn't do. This was just totally selfish human nature.

D. *What was it like being accused of child molestation?*

M. Gut wrenching. My heart stopped. My mind was spinning thinking, well, this won't be that hard to get out of, because there's no hard evidence. That was my initial instinct, but before I admitted that I was guilty, I started realizing that whether I was proven guilty or not, people were going to think I was, because I had been accused. Reality was slow to seep in, but when it did, I started to realize that I had to do the right thing.

D. Describe your experience with the law. What was it like when the police came to the door?

M. Initially I had no idea what was going on, but my heart went into my stomach. They were very professional. I don't think they believed the accusations at all at first, mainly because they were so nice to me. I would have thought that if they had believed it, I would have been incarcerated, at least overnight. But after taking me to the station for an interview, they took me home. They were very good to me. There were two uniformed officers and one plainclothes. They were very professional. I lied through my teeth in the first interview. I was very scared. I think I did a pretty good job of hiding it, but I was scared.

When I went back the second time to confess, it was a huge relief. I felt much, much better about the situation. I finally felt I had done the right thing after a long, long time.

D. What led you to turn yourself in and confess?

M. I realized that this was not going to play out well. That it was going to totally divide the family and betray them more than I already had. By me denying everything, it was more abuse on Sofia. To drag her through a trial was unthinkable. I most likely could have won, if I had played it totally cool and calculated and denied, denied, denied. If I had totally lawyered up and done everything they had told me to do, I could probably have beaten it – but there would have been a big mess in the family and I just really.... I knew I was going away for a long time and I wasn't coming back. I wasn't going to incur any more lawyer's fees for my family. I was just going to plead guilty to everything. I didn't care if I went away for life. I knew the best thing for me to do was admit it. Take the lumps. That was my intent.

D. In case someone who is fantasizing about molesting a child reads this interview, I'd like them to understand the price they'll pay. Could you tell me exactly what happened from the time you turned yourself in?

M. After making my statement, I was put into a holding cell by myself at the O.P.P. station. I was so relieved to finally have the truth out. There was a nice old lady working there and so I started to talk to her and told her how good I felt to have done the right thing. She stood there and asked me what the charges were and I told her. She just went white and became very belligerent and got right on the phone. The constable who I had been talking with came up to my cell and said, "I'm only going to tell you this once. When you go over to the jail, keep your mouth *shut*. People do not want to know about this charge, and so for your own self-preservation, ... And it was very good advice.

But then, when they took me over to the jail, the guards over there already knew. And so all of this stuff started to happen.

D. That lady told them?

M. I don't know. The guards who carry you over have a record of what you're charged with so that they can process you in. So it started with the strip-search with the guards berating me and marching me naked, carrying my jail clothes, in front of everybody in the holding cells with them all yelling at me about how they were going to get me.... I really... I really don't want to go there.

D. Remember, the reason why I'm asking you about the details of this is in hopes that it will be a deterrent to anyone else who is thinking about molesting a child and so that victims will feel that they have had some justice.

M. Yeah. It's hell on earth. You can't believe how alone you are. I basically went nuts for a little while. They

58

psychologically broke me. I was totally delusional for a couple of days at least.

D. What did they do to break you?

M. No sleep. They put me in a padded blanket-garment sort of dress thing with straps made from safety-belt fabric over my shoulders. I was strapped into it. I had no clothes. They had taken everything I had. They control the temperature in the cells and so they turned my heat right down so that it was a very cold cell. All I had was a tiny little blanket about two feet by four feet, made of the same fabric as this dress thing. It was basically what they call their "suicide watch." There was one guard watching me. I don't know his name, but I'll never forget his face. He was a guy who was big in the union and very belligerent. It was that guy who made the decision that I was going to go into the cold cell. I was taken to a nurse and of the corner of my eye I caught him give her a big wink that this was going to happen.

So they kept me there for three days. Basically, they would stay outside my door and taunt me and tell me how terrible I was. They'd carry on conversations outside my door about all the horrible things they'd heard I did. If I did go to sleep at all, they'd bang on my door to make me wake up. So I'd had no sleep at all and was very, very cold for three days.

Then at five in the morning, they took me down to a holding cell to wait until 8:30 to be loaded into a paddy wagon to go to the courthouse. So I was just left there to wait in this absolutely filthy cell. I think they must smear these places with excrement on purpose so that they are as miserable as they can possibly be. The walls are just covered with feces.

D. You mean in the cells below the courthouse?

M. No – in the Super Jail, but the courtroom cells are the same. There are some cells that are okay, and then there are others that are just terrible. When I was first going through all that, I was always put in the worst ones for obvious reasons. It's like a game to some of these people. The worst guards were the women, by far, but in general, there a lot of very, very good people there.

D. *What was the "perp walk?"*

M. After they strip search you, they're supposed to give you an orange jumpsuit with underwear and slippers and you should be able to put those on, because there are five or six low-walled cement cubicles so that when you return from court, you're supposed to strip out of your street clothes back into the prison wear in those cubicles. But instead of that, when a prisoner like me is taken from the holding cell to the regular cells, they make them stay naked, just carrying their prison clothes and walk past all these holding cells, some of which can hold as many as 30 men. Some hold ten or twenty and then there are some cells with just one man. They let these guys know what the charges are and so as I walked down the hall, all these guys were yelling profanities and threats about how they were going to get me. It was .... So that was the perp walk.

D. *So that happened when you first got there?*

M. I turned myself in on Saturday morning and spent Saturday night in a holding cell in the O.P.P. Station. Sunday morning, I did video court from there. Then I was transported to the Super Jail Sunday afternoon and that's where the perp walk and everything else started. That's when I was taken up to the psyche ward and put in the cold cell for three days, supposedly on suicide watch. But every time I was taken back and forth to court, it was like a perp walk because the other prisoners were made aware of what the charges were.

D. Did you ever find yourself in grave danger?

M. Yes. Many times. There were times when I could have been killed – people who wanted to kill me. But God was there and protected me the whole time.

D. You've talked about being active in a church. How could you call yourself a Christian?

M. I had committed my life to God and believed everything in the Bible. I just wasn't following what it said. I put my own desires ahead of everything and didn't work at applying Scripture to my life. I was just a guy sitting in a pew saying all the right things but doing whatever I felt like doing.

Did you feel as though God had left you in prison?

M. No, although I certainly deserved to have Him leave me. There were so many occurrences when really bad things could have happened. I could have died. Just on my pod there were several guys who would have killed me as quick as they would have looked at me if they could have gotten their hands on me. I feel that God gave me wisdom in what to say, what to do and how to react. Whenever I would ask Him what I was to do in a particular situation, I would just feel a flood of peace and I knew He was with me. I'd do whatever it was I felt He told me to do and I was protected.

D. After all of that, do you still have an attraction to children?

M. No. Quite frankly, I've gone overboard the other way. I'm frightened of children now. If I'm in a grocery store and there are a couple of kids in an aisle without their mother, I'll turn my cart around and go the opposite direction. It's just common good sense. It's not that I'm afraid of re-offending, because that's not going to happen. My fear is that I'll be perceived as doing something inappropriate. I'm extremely careful not to put myself in a position where anyone could get the wrong idea.

D. How do you feel about yourself now, generally?

M. I'm just a work in progress. I have difficulty with some things. For instance, in my work, I can't get overly friendly with anybody or invite them to church because if they come to my church, I'll lose my job. Someone there will ask if they know about my background – and that will be it. I'll be history. Any effect I have on people just has to be through the way I live my life, through being a person who is not profane, who is honest and helpful – but I can't invite them to come to my church. And that's just the facts of life. That understanding comes through the first job I got after I was released at a trucking company. I was the best night watchman they had ever had – until one guy found out that I had been in prison and that was it. So it makes that part of it difficult.

D. How do you feel about yourself now in relation to other people?

M. I feel as though I'll always be in a fishbowl. Everybody is reading behind the lines, wondering what I'm doing. I know my pastor and his church board are pleased that I'm doing everything to earn their respect and keep people comfortable and stick to the reintegration plan without being reminded. For instance, I'd never go to the washroom in the church. If I had to go, I'd leave the building and go home and go there. It's just staying way from any perception of acting questionably.

It's difficult because I can't just go out anywhere and socialize and tell anybody about my past and expect anyone to be supportive, because it's just not going to happen. So I'm isolated. I can't just go out and be a normal person. I'm just coming to grips with that now and realizing that that's always the way life is going to be for me. It's my fault – nobody else's.

I do feel very good about my relationship with my parole officer and my psychologist. They are very positive about the support group I have. The fact that my sister and my aunt have been so incredibly supportive says a lot about them and has meant so much to my ability to rebuild my life.

Most of the guys like me don't have the support group I have. They've lost everybody and they just give up. They basically re-offend so that they can go back in to get off the streets. They're without any means and life is just too terrible on the outside.

D. Are you still a manipulator?

M. I don't think so. I hope not. I try to be totally frank and honest about everything and I think that is the key. If someone asks me a direct question, I'm not going to lie about it. For instance, if some one asks me at my work if I have been in prison for child molestation, I'm not about to lie about it. I'll say yes and then I might as well go out and get in my car because I'm going to lose my job. So from that standpoint, I'm not that same person anymore.

I think that's why a few of my old friends and my sister and aunt have stuck by me, because there's been a trust factor built up which I very much cherish. Without it I'd be totally lost. I'd be totally out of my mind, I guess. That's all I can do.

Now, I recognize my lot in life. If I didn't have the backing of my support group, I know I'd be in big trouble. I think I'd just collapse. But I do think that God has brought this support group together. It just seems supernatural to me. I was never that close to my aunt or my sister until this happened.

D. What role does remorse play in your life? How do you deal with the shame?

M. There are realities that I have to live with for the rest of my life. There is an awareness of how deeply this has adversely affected the people in my life. Their woes right now are caused primarily by me and I'm aware of that.

Remorse and shame? This has taught me to see the girls as real people with emotions, thoughts and needs. I betrayed their trust and I feel very badly because I took advantage of their vulnerability.

D. What will you do if the temptation returns?

M. I'm going at life in such a way as to not allow the temptation to return. I've purposed myself to walk away from any possibly compromising situations.

I read a lot and keep myself busy with work and church. When impure thoughts come into my mind, I replace them with positive, healthy thoughts or good memories. The key is not ignoring bad thoughts – it's replacing them. I know that I can talk to my pastor about anything, anytime. We have both come to the conclusion that man, left to his own desires, is very dark. We are all tempted, but left to run rampant, the imagination can be a disastrous thing.

D. So you'd say it's all about renewing the mind?

M. Knowing exactly what the pitfalls are and how to avoid them is critical. Replacing dark thoughts. That's why Philippians Chapter 4 is so important to me. *"Whatever is true, whatever is noble, whatever is right, whatever is pure, whatever is lovely, whatever is admirable – if anything is excellent or praiseworthy – think about such things."* If a temptation comes into my mind, I immediately capture that thought and replace it with something else. Often a memory, like laying on my back, looking up at the stars with one of my grandchildren. That was such a wonderful, solid memory. Or driving down to the lake with my old dog, Jack. The point is that you can't *not* think about something, or it becomes the elephant in the room. It becomes bigger and more important. You have to replace it with something positive. Something better.

D. If you could say anything to your victims, what would it be?

M. That I'm very sorry. I know that sounds like a very trite thing to say. I wish there had been an opportunity for them to confront me – for everyone who this touched to confront me and be able to express how I hurt them. I know that the victim impact statements are meant to do that, but the girls weren't there when I read them. I would like them to know how sorry I truly am. I don't deserve reconciliation, but in the long haul, it is the only thing that will bring peace to them.

D. Is doing this interview an effort on your part to make some restitution?

The best thing I can do for my victims is to never offend again. As the perpetrator, nothing I say means a hill of beans. It's only what I do with the rest of my life that could make some small possible bit of difference to them. I'm aware of that. It may never any difference and that thought makes me very sad, but it's a true thought. It's a reality.

D. Is there anything I haven't asked?

M. There are no excuses for anyone to molest a child. No reasons. Every individual is responsible for his or her own choices. Mine were detestably self-gratifying. The road to healing starts with taking responsibility for your own actions. All of the repercussions I face were brought on by my own hand. They are no one else's fault.

D. What would you say to someone who was just on the edge, was fooling around with pornography, hadn't touched a child yet, but was fantasizing about doing it? Knowing what you know now, what warning could you give a potential molester that could deter them from sexually interfering with a child?

M. It's a tough situation because, from a self-preservation standpoint, there's nowhere for the potential perpetrator to go without severe repercussions. If he hasn't touched a child yet, there hasn't been any law broken, but to go to anyone to discuss it, he would have to be very careful that it was the right person. But the reality is that if you do it, you're eventually going to get caught. Look at all these old priests, 70 and 80 years old who thought they'd gotten away with it all those years, but then the victims started to tell.

D. What if they've already molested a child?

If something has actually happened, people who know about it are bound by law to identify predators and predators have to come to the conclusion that they will have to accept the consequences. They will have to pay the price, one way or another.

The thing is that if you've done something, in the grand scheme of things, you want to hope that you get caught on this side of eternity. If it doesn't come out until the other side of eternity, there's no chance to make anything right and you'll have to suffer in torment forever. You're done. There is no hope. Ever. You've got to get help. You've got to stop.

The good thing about facing the music, if there is a good part, is that they can stop themselves from hurting another child and they can have a second chance at eternity. For those who want to rebuild their lives and change, there's a good possibility that they may find a support group and the respect of mature Christians who will nurture them along in their battle.

I'm a living testament to that. I went from having a nice middle-class life with all the amenities; you know, a family, nice cars, big house, a half-decent business that kept us going for many years – to absolutely nothing. But I'm better now than I was with all that, because with a strong support group, I'm finally living an honest life.

I went to the first job I could find after getting out of prison – as a night watchman for a trucking company. I did well – got a raise far before I was supposed to get a raise – then they found out I'd been in prison and boom – they let me go. I was emotionally devastated.

If molesters turn themselves in, eventually they have to realize that there is a certain segment of society that will never forgive them, no matter how well they try to do. There are those that already have and then there are those who may eventually be able to forgive.

But until something actually happens, there's still the chance of getting help. If I had known (Pastor) Rob, I could have talked to him.

D. Would you have?

M. Most likely not. In all honesty, probably not. But I could have because he's a guy you could reach out to who would make you accountable and get you help. And that's what you need. You can't just think, well I'm going to fix this, because you can't.

With all the therapy I've had now, I've found that there's a lot of secular garbage out there that just doesn't work. Undoubtedly it does help some people, but it's all about self-help and that doesn't always work because sometimes you need help beyond yourself. Secular fixes are all over the map. There are places that will tell you that pornography is a good thing, that it helps you get release – get into pornography so that you don't molest someone – but it's like – hello!

D. These are treatment places that are telling you this?

M. Well you know there are some that say, why don't you just go and get release with some porn instead of molesting a child. That mind set is out there and it's perpetrated by the porn industry, because it's a multi-billion dollar industry and that's the bottom line. The buck. And it's not just sleaze bags producing it. Media conglomerates that everyone thinks of as reputable are actually bankrolling these things. You listen to the lyrics on MTV. I'd name the sponsors but I don't want to get you sued. Everybody knows who they are anyway. This is the stuff kids are feeding on.

D. How has your experience in jail changed you?

M. It has changed me in a lot of ways. I used to be a "lock 'em up and throw away the key" kind of guy in terms of my regard for people who were convicted of crimes. After being in jail, I've seen a different side. I've seen a very sad side to society. We're not handling those we incarcerate properly. About 80 percent of people in there are in for drug-related offences. They're under-achievers who never had a chance. Their family backgrounds are horrific and we're not training them to do anything but be better criminals. We're throwing them in with really hardened types and so whatever they're doing criminally, they're just learning to do better.

There need to be mentoring programs and a technical training atmosphere. I think in some areas of the jail there are some facilities like that, but where I was, there was nothing like that at all.

Another old fellow and I spent hours and hours helping young men write letters to parole boards and things. I was never the greatest writer or speller, but it actually helped me to become a better wordsmith and speller because I got a dictionary from the canteen and used it all the time. These guys were sooo appreciative to have someone help them. Many of them were totally illiterate. It changed me in terms of having compassion for people in tough situations.

Some of them are in the right place, but with others, it was just circumstances that got them there.

People like the pastor who I met in there and a former neighbor who visits people in prison, are like gold in the prison. My old neighbor is an amazing woman. On the other hand, there were some chaplains in there who were a joke. They don't believe God can change people and do nothing to give them hope. It really made me appreciate people who are working quietly behind the scenes to try to change peoples lives.

Another thing that changed was my appreciation for the people who stood by me. I don't hold any animosity towards those who didn't stand by me. The important thing was the ones that stood by me. It certainly gave me more of an appreciation for the things that are important in life.

D. And what are those?

M. Living the best life you can live and being content with that. Being content with plenty and being content in difficult circumstances. I've found that God really does provide for our needs. It's wonderful not to have anxiety.

There's really nothing I fear anymore, because all the great fears in life, I've been brought through and God sustained me and protected me in situations that were untenable and uncontrollable from my standpoint. I have a great assurance that He is in control and I can go through anything now.

Another thing I've learned is about staying in God's Word. There's a booklet that I now get quarterly called, *The Word for You Today*. It was first given to me in prison. Bob and Debby Gass, who write it, must really hear from God, because it's sometimes just like reading a right-on horoscope. It so often speaks to the very thing that I'm experiencing that very day. It's awesome.

D. How do you feel about yourself now, generally?

M. I'm basically having to be content with the situation. And that can be very difficult because I will always be very lonely. I see myself as the guy with the scarlet letter. It's just a fact of life – something that I will always have to deal with. I'm very grateful that the majority of the people in the church are on side with me. As long as I keep my nose clean they will support me, so that's a good thing.

D. How do you feel about your family – not seeing your sons or grandkids?

M. That is my biggest, my major concern. But I have come to realize that I have no control over it. I cannot force that issue.

I totally understand the betrayal. My deepest prayer is that they will one day be able to forgive me for the way I have ruined so many lives.

I think that part of their pain goes far beyond what I did. I never fathered the boys the way I should have. The fact that I didn't have the skills because my father didn't father me was no excuse. I never, never remember having a loving conversation with my dad, but I should have been digging in to books by Dr. Dobson and other parenting experts and finding out how to do it right, but I was so selfish and preoccupied that I didn't pay attention.

D. What about your relationship with God. Do you feel that you had an authentic Christian conversion in the beginning?

M. Yes. It was authentic. But I slid backwards.

D. How has your relationship with Him changed?

M. He is all I have now. I came to terms with Him before I went to jail, at the same time that I determined that I had to do the right thing and confess. Ever since, I've felt that there are no walls between me and God. I can be real with Him.

D. What would you say to all those men who are sitting in church pews or living otherwise respectable lives but logging on to porn sites when no one is around?

M. They need some accountability. They need people around them who can bring them up on the carpet on anything. And those men they want to select very carefully. A man needs an accountability group around him until the day he dies – at least one man, preferably two or more.

D. How would you have handled all of this without God?

M. I most likely would have killed myself.

D. *Before or after you were caught?*

M. After.

D. *At what point?*

M. Most likely the first couple of weeks in prison.

D. *So why didn't you?*

M. Because I came to the conclusion, with the Chaplain's help, that it would have just been another abuse. It would have been another very selfish act, because at some point in their lives, Sofia or Lucas might have thought that if they hadn't turned me in, I'd still be alive. And they did the right thing, so I have no right to put any guilt on them. Suicide is just another form of abuse, just another manipulation, another scheme and I can't do that. It's a very hurtful scheme because you can't ever communicate with the person again. It's a total cop out. Not a brave thing to do. It's a very immature thing.

D. *How did you sit in church on Sundays and listen to Christian radio and yet maintain your interest in pornography?*

M. Again, the self gratification outweighed my spiritual walk. I was weak spiritually. I think every man has the potential for giving in to pornography and if they do, they just gradually deteriorate. It may take hours, days, weeks, months or years – but if you play with fire, you're going to get burned.

I believe the only way to stay clear is by feeding on the actual Word of God. Listening to great preachers or reading books may be good, but that's not it. It can be helpful – Dr. Stanley really helped me from time to time. But there's nothing that replaces the Word of God. Philippians, Chapter Four, was very important to me. It's like the oil that makes everything work right. If you can stay grounded in Scripture, you have hope. It's the key to success. If you try to wean away from it, you're in trouble. It's got to be first place. It's got to be priority job one. Knowing that for the rest of your life is extremely important. It gives a peace that you can't get anywhere else.

D. How about the contention that people in your circumstances just get "jailhouse religion?"

M. That's often true. Many of the fellows in prison had exactly that. Their visits to the chaplain were all about ulterior motives. They wanted to be regarded well by parole boards or whatever. I knew when I was writing some of these letters that I was being used – so for those people I tried to write even better letters, because it wasn't my job to judge their hearts. God has a purpose. While I was in there, I was supposed to help those fellows in any way I could. I did a lot of it.

D. How do you feel about the institution of marriage now?

M. Unless a marriage is built on total trust and honesty, it's not going to work. The relationship has to be so intimate that you can tell the person your deepest darkest secrets and know that they won't reject you. I think there are marriages like that, but I think that the majority of people are just going through the motions. I do see the occasional phenomenal one, but I think that transparency and honesty are more important than love.

D. I am afraid I'll come under fire for not being more observant. For not realizing what was going on.

M. You can't shoulder that, because you were deceived. It's like the way the German people believed in Hitler. You know, a whole nation of people. They were duped and that's exactly what happened with you. You weren't living with reality. It wasn't a fair situation. It wasn't a balanced situation you were having to deal with. I think you did everything to the very best of your ability. I never knew you to shirk your responsibilities. I always was so amazed at how patient and diligent you were in raising the kids and living by your principles, sticking by your guns. There were so many admirable traits to your character that I would see time and time again that were amazing. You were an amazing person. You're still an amazing person. You'll always be an amazing person to me. I have to focus on the good times out of those years and not the bad times. I get depressed enough without getting into.... Depression is an extremely destructive thing and I'm sure you feel that sometimes, too. But I can't stay in it. I've got to talk to somebody. Get out of it. Run, don't walk. It's totally counter-productive. Totally soul destroying. It doesn't allow a person to function at all.

D. How do you feel about yourself now?

M. I like myself a lot more than I did. There's not much left of me, but what's there is honest. And I have real feelings for people. I feel a warmth with people that I didn't feel before. Like when I'm with Rob, I just really like him. I hate to say goodbye. It's different now.

❧

Update

It has been over 18 years since Matt's confession. Although the family is still broken, I see God at work, healing the victims and my sons, step by step. I dismantled our business, sold our home and, at the age of 60, went back to school and registered ByDesign Media *www.bydesignmedia.ca* a year to the day following Matt's confession. I have dedicated my life to the protection of children by whatever means and through whatever opportunities present themselves. My desire is to spotlight any areas of darkness that could enable child-molesters to continue to harm children; helping parents, grandparents and caregivers to keep them safe – and to raise awareness with regard to the development of inclinations in people to molest children.

Believing in the tenets of Restorative Justice, I visited Matt in prison and assisted him in his reintegration into the community. Because the best way to ensure there will be no re-offending rests on the true transformation of the inner person, my hope has been that he will continue to grow in his relationship with God and with supportive friends. He has remarried but does not see his family.

In 2021, I married Glen Rutledge, founder of the Circle Square TV and Circle Square Ranches, through which over 250,000 kids (including mine) were shown the love of Jesus and provided with a strong foundation for their lives. Together we have been building *LifeNet Ministries Inc.* in response to the vision God gave Glen for reaching vulnerable young people through social media. As a suicide prevention program, we now have a call centre/prayer line that covers the US and Canada, and are making inroads into Mexico, Costa Rica and England and wherever God opens doors. Because the majority of kids who commit suicide have been abused, with this series we are working to make a preemptive strike against tragedy. Please join us with your support.

www.lifenet4hope.com

For further reading...

Abel, G., Becker, J., Mittleman, M., Rouleau, J., and Murphy, W. (1987)Journal of Interpersonal Violence, 2(1), March

Beauregard, M and O'Leary, D. (2007). *The Spiritual Brain*, A Neuroscientist's Case for the Existence of the Soul, HarperOne, San Francisco, CA

The Holy Bible, The New International Version, Zondervan Bible Publishers, Grand Rapids, Michigan

Birchall, E. (1989). The Frequency of Child Abuse – What do We Really Know?, in Colton, Matthew and Vanstone, Maurice (1996). *Betrayal of Trust*; Sexual Abuse by Men Who Work With Children, London ON: Free Association Books Ltd.

Bremner, Dr. J. Douglas (2007). The Lasting Effects of Psychological Trauma on Memory and the Hippocampus, Law and Psychiatry

Briggs, F., & Hawkins, R.M.F. (1996). A comparison of the childhood experiences of convicted male child molesters and men who were sexually abused in childhood and claimed to be non offenders. *Child Abuse and Neglect*

Browne, A., & Finkelhor, D. (1986). Initial and long-term effects: A review of the research. In D. Finkelhor, *A Sourcebook on Child Sexual Abuse*, Beverly Hills: Sage

Bushman, B.J., Baumeister, R.F., & Stack, A.D. (1999). Catharsis, aggression and persuasive influence: Self-fulfilling or self-defeating prophecies? Journal of Personality and Social Psychology

Butler, Sandra (1985). *Conspiracy of Silence: The Trauma of Incest*, San Francisco, Volcano Press

Carnes, Patrick (1994). *Out of the Shadows*; Understanding Sexual Addiction, Center City, Minnesota: Hazelden Foundation

Carter, Wm. Lee (2002). *A Teen's Guide to Overcoming Sexual Abuse;* It Happened to Me, Oakland, Ca., New Harbinger Publications, Inc.

Colton, Matthew and Vanstone, Maurice (1996). *Betrayal of Trust*; Sexual Abuse by Men Who Work With Children, , London ON: Free Association Books Ltd.

Diagnostic and Statistical Manual of Mental Disorders (DSM 111-R), The American Psychological Association, 1987

Elliott, M., Browne, K., & Kilcoyne, J. (1995). *Child Sexual Abuse Prevention: What Offenders Tell Us*, Child Abuse & Neglect

Finkelhor, D. (1984). *Child Sexual Abuse: New Theory and Research*, New York: Free Press

Finkelhor, D. and associates (eds) (1986), *A Sourcebook on Child Sexual Abuse*, Newbury Park, CA.: Sage

Finkelhor, D., Hotaling, G., Lewis, I. and Smith, C. (1990) *Sexual Abuse in a National Survey of Adult Men and Women;* Prevalence Characteristics and Risk Factors, *Child Abuse and Neglect*

Finkelhor, D. (1994). The International epidemiology of child sexual abuse. *Child Abuse & Neglect*, 18

Finkelhor, D. and Dziuba-Leatherman, J. (1995). Victimization prevention programs: A national survey of children's exposure and reactions, *Child Abuse & Neglect*

Finney, Lynne D. (1992). *Reach for the Rainbow*; Advance Healing for Survivors of Sexual Abuse, New York: The Putnam Publishing Group

Forward, Susan, and Craig Buck (1979). *Betrayal of Innocence: Incest and its Devastation*, New York: Penguin Books

Genesee Justice Family (2005). *Genesee Justice 2005*; Instruments of Law, Order and Peace, Batavia, N.Y., Genesee Justice Family Research & Development

Groth, N., Burgess, A., Birnbaum, H. and Gary, T. (1978). A study of the child molester. Myths and realities. *LAE Journal of the American Criminal Justice Association*, 41(1), Winter/Spring

Halliday, L. (1985). *Sexual Abuse:* Counseling issues and concerns. Campbell River, B.C., Ptarmigan Press

Hergenhahn, B.R. (1992). *An Introduction to the History of Psychology*. Belmont, CA:Wadsworth Publishing Company

Hopper, Dr. J. (2007). Child Abuse: Statistics, Research and Resources Jacob Wetterling Foundation web site's frequently asked questions section

Knopp, Fay Honey (1982). *Remedial Intervention in Adolescent Sex Offenses*; Nine Program Descriptions, Brooklyn, N.Y.: Faculty Press, Inc.

Leaf , Dr. Caroline (2007). *Who Switched Off My Brain?*, Switch on Your Brain, Rivonia, South Africa

Lilienfeld, Scott O. and Lambert, Kelly (Oct. 2007). Brain Stains, Scientific American

MacAulay, The Honourable Lawrence - Solicitor General Canada (2001). *High-Risk Offenders; A Handbook for Criminal Justice Professionals,* Ottawa, The Government of Canada

Marshall, Dr. W.L. and Barrett, Sylvia (1990). *Criminal Neglect*; Why Sex Offenders Go Free, Toronto: Doubleday Canada Limited

Matthews, Dr. Frederick (1995). *Breaking Silence - Creating Hope*; Help for Adults Who Molest Children, Ottawa: National Clearinghouse on Family Violence, Health Canada

McCoy, D. (2006). *The Manipulative Man*, Adams Media, Avon, Mass.

Mercy, J. A. (1999). *Having New Eyes:* Viewing Child Sexual Abuse as a Public Health Problem. Sexual Abuse: A Journal of Research and Treatment

Michel, Lou and Herbeck, Dan, *Confessions of a Child Porn Addict,* The Buffalo News, Oct. 21, 2007

Minnery, Tom (1986). *Pornography; A Human Tragedy*, Wheaton, Illinois, Tyndale House Publishers Inc., Dr. J. Dobson

Murr, Doris C. (2004). *Dorie's Secret*, Kitchener, Ontario, Pandora Press

Peck, M. Scott (1983). People of the Lie, New York, Touchstone - Simon & Schuster Inc.

Posten, Carol and Lison, Karen (1990). *Reclaiming our Lives*; Hope for Adult Survivors of Incest, Boston, MA: Little, Brown & Company

Pryor, Douglas W. (1996). *Unspeakable Acts*; Why men Sexually Abuse Children, New York and London: New York University Press

Public Health Agency of Canada (2007), National Clearinghouse on Family Violence.

Reavill, Gil (2005). *Smut;* A Sex Industry Insider (and Concerned father) says Enough is Enough, London, England, Penguin Books, Ltd.

Rush, F. (1980). *The Best Kept Secret: Sexual abuse of children.* New York, McGraw-Hill Book Company

Salter, Anna C. (1988). *Treating Child Sex Offenders and Victims*; A Practical Guide, Newbury Park, California: SAGE Publications, Inc.

Salter, Anna C. (2003). *Predators: Pedophiles, Rapists and Other Sex Offenders* , New York: Basic Books

Science Daily, July 30, 2007. News release issued by Stanford University Medical Centre

Seligman, M.E.P. (1994). *What You Can Change and What You Can't.* New York: Alfred A. Knopf

Sher, Julian (2007). *One Child at a Time,* Random House Canada

Singer, P. (1991). Ethics. *The New Encyclopedia Britannica*, Volume 18, Edition 15

UN Secretary General's Study on Violence Against Children (2006) section II.B

Van Dam, Carla (2001). *Identifying Child Molesters, Preventing Child Sexual Abuse by Recognizing the Patterns of the Offenders,* New York: The Halworth Maltreatment and Trauma Press

Wholey, Sam (1992). *When the Worst That Can Happen Already Has*; Conquering Life's Most Difficult Times, New York: Hyperion

Yantzi, Mark (1998). *Sexual Offending and Restoration*, Waterloo, Ontario and Scottdale, Pa., Herald Press

For further information on

LifeNet Ministries Inc.
Youth Suicide Prevention
1-855-691-5350   *www.lifenet4hope.com*

Plan to Protect® Inc.
Training Workshops and Speakers
Information and Training Materials, please contact:
117 Ringwood Dr. Unit #11. Stouffville, ON L4A 8C1.
www.plantoprotect.com   905-642-4693 Toll-Free: 1-877-455-3555

*Plan to Protect® provides the HIGHEST STANDARD of
abuse prevention and protection to organizations and
individuals servicing the vulnerable sector.*

Diane Roblin-Lee
diane@bydesignmedia.ca
www.bydesignmedia.ca

*The 9-Booklet Series, Predator-Proof Your Family
is on Amazon in both Kindle and Paperback Format*

www.ingramcontent.com/pod-product-compliance
Lightning Source LLC
Chambersburg PA
CBHW070837050426
42452CB00011B/2318